Tough Topics

# *Bullying*

Elizabeth Raum

Heinemann Library
Chicago, Illinois

Customer Service  888-454-2279

Visit our website at www.heinemannlibrary.com

Designed by Joanna Hinton-Malivoire
Photo research by Tracy Cummins
Printed in China by South China Printing.

12 11 10 09 08
10 9 8 7 6 5 4 3 2 1

**Library of Congress Cataloging-in-Publication Data**
Raum, Elizabeth.
  Bullying / Elizabeth Raum.
    p. cm. --  (Tough topics)
  Includes bibliographical references and index.
  ISBN-13: 978-1-4329-0818-8 (hc), ISBN-10: 1-4329-0818-9 (hc)
  ISBN-13: 978-1-4329-0823-2 (pb), ISBN-10: 1-4329-0823-5 (pb)
  1.  Bullying--Juvenile literature. 2.  Conduct of life--Juvenile literature.  I. Title.
  BF637.B85R38 2008
  302.3--dc22
                                    2007033266

**Acknowledgments**
The author and publisher are grateful to the following for permission to reproduce copyright material: ©Corbis pp. 7 (Michael Prince), 11 (Norbert Schaefer), 13 (zefa/Heide Benser), 16 (Kevin Dodge), 17 (Creasource), 18, 23 (Royalty Free), 20 (Little Blue Wolf Productions/Royalty Free), 25 (zefa/M. Thomsen), 28 (Najlah Feanny); ©Getty Images pp. 6, 8, 9, 26, 29 (Royalty Free), 10 (Matt Henry Gunther), 12 (Catherine Ledner), 19 (David Roth), 21 (John Giustina), 24 (DreamPictures), 27 (Robert Burke); ©Jupiter Images p. 4 (Corbis/Royalty Free); ©Masterfile pp. 5 (Royalty Free), 15 (Raoul Minsart); ©SuperStock p. 22 (BilderLounge).

Cover photograph reproduced with permission of ©Jupiter Images/Corbis.

Every effort has been made to contact copyright holders of any material reproduced in this book. Any omissions will be rectified in subsequent printings if notice is given to the publisher.

The author would like to thank Ms. Helen Scully, Guidance Counselor, Central Elementary School, Warren Township, New Jersey, for her valuable assistance.

# Contents

Some words are shown in bold, **like this**. You can find out what they mean by looking in the Glossary.

# What Is Bullying?

**Bullying** is hurting, scaring, or leaving someone out on purpose. Bullying is unkind and unfair. Bullying hurts everyone.

▶No one wants to be bullied.

▼Bullying can cause hurt feelings.

Children may meet **bullies** at school or in their neighborhoods. Many children are bullied. Other children worry when they see bullies hurting others. They may not know how to help.

▲Sometimes bullies form a gang.

Both boys and girls can be bullies. Bullies may hit, shove, or kick. They may call others names or make mean jokes about the way a child looks or acts.

Bullying also includes leaving someone out, **gossiping**, or being mean to another child. Bullies can act alone or in a group. Bullying hurts. No one wants to be laughed at or left out.

It hurts to be left out.

# What If I'm Bullied?

It's scary to be bullied. Remind yourself that you are a good person. You don't deserve to be treated badly. No one does.

▼Every person is special. No one should be bullied.

▶ Stand tall. It makes you look **confident**.

Bullies sometimes pick on children who are quiet and don't stand up for themselves. But, anyone can be bullied.

▲ Try to smile when you face the bully. It helps you feel brave.

Act brave even if you are scared. Bullies want to make you cry. If you act as if the **teasing** doesn't bother you, the bully may give up.

Look directly at the bully. Then walk quickly toward an adult you trust. It's important to tell someone if you are being bullied.

▼Look the bully in the eyes. This tells the bully that you are not afraid.

# How to Stay Safe

Stay away from the bully. Join a group of children or stand by the teacher. If you are worried, tell a teacher.

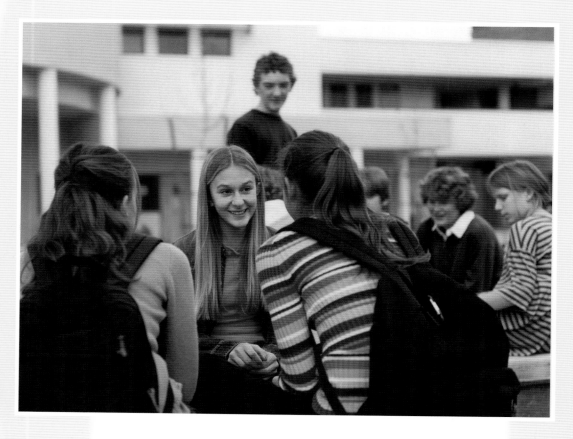

▲Bullies are not likely to bother you if you are in a group.

Don't try to make the bully angry.
Don't call the bully names or hit back.
It just gives the bully a reason to
**attack** you.

◀ Hitting back
is a bad idea.

## Tips for Dealing with Bullies

➔ Be confident. Speak up for yourself.

➔ Play in a group or near a teacher.

➔ Yell if you need help.

➔ Walk away. Don't fight back.

➔ Tell a teacher or other helpful adult that you are being bullied.

Bullies might say things that make you feel bad. Tell yourself that the things the bully says about you aren't true. Say, "I like who I am."

◄ Yell loudly. Bullies don't want teachers to see what they are doing.

If a bully keeps bothering you, yell loudly. Shout "Stop that!" or "Help!" and run to get a teacher or playground aide. Tell him or her what happened.

# Make Yourself Bully-Proof

It is very important to stay away from the bully. Stay with a group of friends. Bullies often pick on children who are alone.

▲You are safer with a group.

▲Friends make you feel stronger.

Find other children who look friendly.
When you find children you think you
can trust, smile. Say "Hello." Join their
games.  Share your lunch. Be a friend to
them, and they will be friends to you.

◄ Make sure you feel safe on the way home.

If you walk to school, walk home with a friend. If you take a bus, sit near the driver. Sit beside someone you trust.

Stick up for yourself. Shout if something is wrong. Yell if you feel scared. Adults need to know if you are being bullied so that they can help you.

▼ Always let people know if you need help.

# What If I See Bullying?

If you see someone being bullied, don't watch. Don't cheer. Yell, "Stop that!" or "Help!" Then run for help. Tell a teacher what is happening.

▲ Run for help.

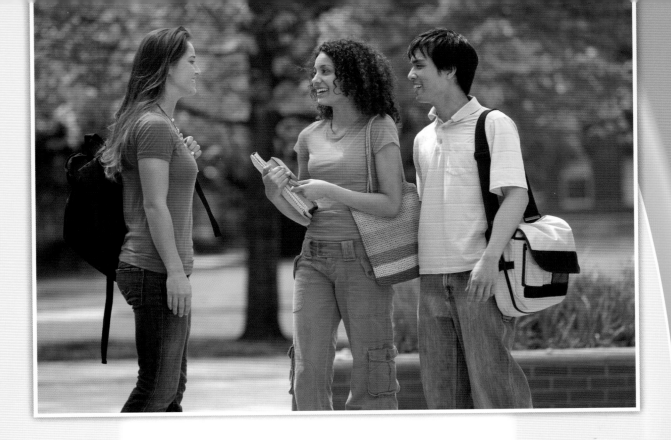

▲ Make room in your group of friends for others.

When the danger is past, be kind to the **victim**. Be sure to include him or her in games. Bullies don't usually pick on groups of people.

# Am I a Bully?

▲ Children don't want to spend time with someone who scares them.

Most children think that bullies are mean and unkind. They don't look up to bullies. Most children stay away from bullies.

▼Many bullies get into trouble.

Bullies need help, too. Many bullies are sad and lonely. Bullies will feel better about themselves when they learn to be kind to others.

▲ Young children respect those
who help them.

If you are a bully, practice being nice to
others. Be kind to younger children.
When others see you doing something
good, they will begin to change how
they think of you.

◄ Many bullies are smart. They can become class leaders.

Most bullies pick on others to feel better about themselves. There are better ways to make yourself feel good. Ask a parent or teacher for help.

# Talk to an Adult

Bullying is a big problem. School should be a safe place. Talk to your teacher or principal if you are worried about bullying at your school.

▲ These children feel safe at school.

▲ Teachers want to help.

Telling a teacher or principal about bullying is important. Telling helps to keep you and other children safe. You are not telling to get the bully in trouble. You are telling to keep everyone from **harm**.

▲ This school does not allow bullying.

Some schools have programs to stop bullying. If your school does not have a bully **prevention** program, ask your principal to start one. Every school should be a safe school.

▲ School should be a safe place for everyone.

You can follow these three rules to make school a safer, happier place for everyone:
- I will not bully other students.
- I will try to help students who are bullied.
- I will include students who may be left out.

# Glossary

**attack** fight

**bully** someone who hurts, scares, or leaves someone out on purpose

**bullying** when one person hurts, scares, or leaves someone out on purpose

**confident** sure of yourself

**gossip** unkind talk about other people

**harm** hurt

**prevention** stopping something from happening

**tease** make fun of someone

**victim** someone who is hurt or harmed

# Find Out More

## Books to Read

Bateman, Teresa. *The Bully Blockers Club*. Morton Grove, IL: Albert Whitman, 2004.

McCain, Becky Ray. *Nobody Knew What To Do: A Story About Bullying*. Morton Grove, IL: Albert Whitman, 2001.

Sanders, Bruce. *Let's Talk About Bullying*. Mankato, MN: Stargazer, 2006.

Shapiro, Lawrence E. *Betty Stops the Bully: An Emotional Literacy Book*. Warrenton, VA: CTC Publishing, 2006.

## Websites

- Pacer.org (http://www.pacerkidsagainstbullying.org/) is a Website that helps kids understand bullying.

- Talk-helps.com (http://www.talk-helps.com/) helps kids avoid bullying through practice exercises.

# Index